The Morristown &
Morris Township Library
1 Miller Road
Morristown NJ 07960

the
Living
Ocean

Wonderful Whales

Bobbie Kalman

Crabtree Publishing Company

www.crabtreebooks.com

Created by Bobbie Kalman

For my friend Tony Dempsey,
who loves Quantum Physics *almost* as much as I do!

Editor-in-Chief
Bobbie Kalman

Writing team
Bobbie Kalman
Hadley Dyer

Substantive editors
Kelley MacAulay
Kathryn Smithyman

Editors
Molly Aloian
Robin Johnson
Reagan Miller

Design
Margaret Amy Salter
Samantha Crabtree (cover)

Production coordinator
Heather Fitzpatrick

Photo research
Crystal Foxton

Consultant
Patricia Loesche, Ph.D., Animal Behavior Program,
Department of Psychology, University of Washington

Illustrations
Barbara Bedell: pages 5 (all except polar bear), 6 (all except pygmy right whale),
    7 (all except Hector's dolphin), 10-11, 14 (krill), 26-27 (humpback whale, krill, orca, and squid)
Jeannette McNaughton-Julich: page 17
Trevor Morgan: pages 26-27 (harp seal)
Vanessa Parson-Robbs: pages 6 (pygmy right whale), 26-27 (anchovies)
Bonna Rouse: page 14 (mackerel)
Margaret Amy Salter: back cover, pages 5 (polar bear), 14 (magnifying glass and plankton),
    26-27 (background, clams, lobster, magnifying glass, and plankton)
Tiffany Wybouw: pages 7 (Hector's dolphin), 11 (baleen plate), 20 (top), 25,
    26-27 (pacific white-sided dolphin)

Photographs and reproductions
Robert Thomas: front cover (art reproduction)
Bobbie Kalman: page 12 (right)
SeaPics.com: ©Phillip Colla: page 24; ©Bob Cranston: page 15 (bottom);
    ©David B. Fleetham: title page; ©John K. B. Ford/Ursus: page 16;
    ©Michael S. Nolan: pages 22, 31; ©Doug Perrine: pages 4, 9, 20 (left);
    ©Doc White: page 15 (top)
The Whale Center of New England: page 14
Other images by Corbis, Corel, Digital Stock, and Digital Vision

Crabtree Publishing Company

www.crabtreebooks.com   1-800-387-7650

Copyright © **2006 CRABTREE PUBLISHING COMPANY**.
All rights reserved. No part of this publication may be
reproduced, stored in a retrieval system or be transmitted in
any form or by any means, electronic, mechanical, photocopying,
recording, or otherwise, without the prior written permission
of Crabtree Publishing Company. In Canada: We acknowledge
the financial support of the Government of Canada through
the Book Publishing Industry Development Program (BPIDP)
for our publishing activities.

Cataloging-in-Publication Data
Kalman, Bobbie.
    Wonderful whales / Bobbie Kalman.
        p. cm. -- (The living ocean series)
    Includes index.
    ISBN-13: 978-0-7787-1302-9 (rlb)
    ISBN-10: 0-7787-1302-4 (rlb)
    ISBN-13: 978-0-7787-1324-1 (pbk)
    ISBN-10: 0-7787-1324-5 (pbk)
    1. Whales--Juvenile literature. I. Title. II. Series.
    QL737.C4K2556 2005
    599.5--dc22
                                2005022994
                                LC

**Published in
the United States**
PMB16A
350 Fifth Ave.
Suite 3308
New York, NY
10118

**Published
in Canada**
616 Welland Ave.,
St. Catharines, Ontario
Canada
L2M 5V6

**Published in the
United Kingdom**
73 Lime Walk
Headington
Oxford
OX3 7AD
United Kingdom

**Published
in Australia**
386 Mt. Alexander Rd.,
Ascot Vale (Melbourne)
VIC 3032

Contents

Ocean mammals

Whales are **mammals**. Mammals are **vertebrates**, or animals that have backbones. Whales are **warm-blooded**. The bodies of warm-blooded animals stay about the same temperature, whether their surroundings are warm or cold.

Like all mammals, whales have lungs for breathing air. Mammal mothers produce milk in their bodies for their babies to drink. Most mammals have fur or hair on their bodies, but whales have only a few whiskers on their snouts.

Whales have been living on Earth for thousands of years. The whales above are humpback whales.

Marine mammals

Whales belong to a group of mammals called **marine mammals**. Marine mammals live mainly in oceans. Some marine mammals, such as whales, sea otters, manatees, and dugongs, live only in oceans. Other marine mammals, including polar bears, seals, sea lions, and walruses, live both in water and on land.

A polar bear finds its food mainly in the ocean.

A sea lion has front and back flippers. It can turn its back flippers forward and "walk" on land.

*A sea otter lives only in shallow **coastal** waters.*

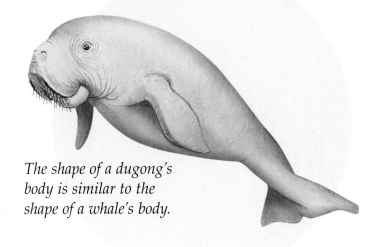

The shape of a dugong's body is similar to the shape of a whale's body.

5

Whale species

There are about 84 **species**, or types, of whales. These species make up a large group of marine mammals called **cetaceans**. Scientists divide cetaceans into two subgroups: **baleen whales** and **toothed whales**. Species that belong to the same subgroup often have bodies that are similar shapes, sizes, and colors. Each species is also different in certain ways.

Baleen whales

The baleen whale subgroup includes about thirteen species of whales. These species are divided into four family groups: **gray whales**, **right whales**, **pygmy right whales**, and **rorqual whales**.

Gray whales make up their own family group. Gray whales have scars and bumps on their bodies.

*There are four species of right whales. North Atlantic right whales are **endangered**.*

Pygmy right whales also make up their own family group. They are the smallest baleen whales.

The blue whale is one of seven species of rorqual whales. It is the biggest animal on Earth! It can grow to be longer than 100 feet (30 m) and to weigh more than 35 tons (32,000 kg).

Toothed whales

There are about 71 species of toothed whales. Dolphins and porpoises belong to the toothed whale subgroup, but they are not usually called whales. There are ten family groups of toothed whales. These ten groups are divided into three **superfamilies**. Dolphins, porpoises, narwhals, and beluga whales make up one superfamily. Beaked whales and sperm whales each make up their own superfamily.

Hector's dolphins are the smallest cetaceans. They are just under four feet (1.2 m) long.

A male narwhal has a long tooth that sticks out from the front of its head. This tooth is mainly hollow inside.

*Porpoises look similar to dolphins. Unlike dolphins, porpoises have rounded heads, and they do not have **beaks**, or long snouts, as dolphins do.*

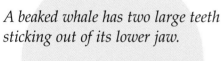

A beaked whale has two large teeth sticking out of its lower jaw.

Beluga whales are the only whales that are white.

Sperm whales are the largest toothed whales.

7

Where do whales live?

Whales live in ocean **habitats** all around the world. A habitat is the natural place where an animal lives. Whales live in all three types of oceans: warm **tropical oceans**, icy **polar oceans**, and **temperate oceans**. Temperate oceans are found in parts of the world where the seasons change. These oceans are warm in summer and cold in winter.

Warm or cold?

Some species of whales live only in tropical oceans or polar oceans. The vaquita is a porpoise that lives only in tropical waters. Other species of whales can live in either warm oceans or cold oceans. Orcas can be found living in all three types of oceans. The orcas in the picture live in a polar ocean.

Home range

Most whale species have **home ranges**. A whale's home range is the area of the ocean in which the whale lives and finds food. Some species of whales have small home ranges. For example, certain bottlenose dolphins stay within a range of 48 square miles (124 km^2). Other whales have large home ranges. Minke whales have home ranges as large as 232 square miles (601 km^2).

Different depths

The home ranges of some whales are in shallow waters close to shore. Many species of dolphins and baleen whales live close to shore. Other whales live in deep ocean waters, which are far from shore. Some whales that live far from shore dive deep in the ocean. For example, sperm whales can dive thousands of feet beneath the surface of the ocean!

*Some whales, such as this bottlenose dolphin, have home ranges in the shallow, tropical waters around **coral reefs**. Coral reefs are large underwater structures that are made up of corals.*

A whale's body

Different species of whales have bodies that are different shapes, sizes, and colors. All whales have many body parts in common, however. Whale bodies are suited for life in oceans. They are **fusiform**, or torpedo-shaped. Having torpedo-shaped bodies helps whales move easily through water. Mammals have fur or hair on their bodies to keep them warm, but whales have almost none. Instead, whales have thick layers of **blubber**, or fat, on their bodies. Blubber traps heat and keeps whales warm in cold waters. Blubber also helps whales stay **buoyant**, or afloat, in water. Blubber is lighter than muscle is, so having a lot of blubber on their bodies helps whales stay afloat.

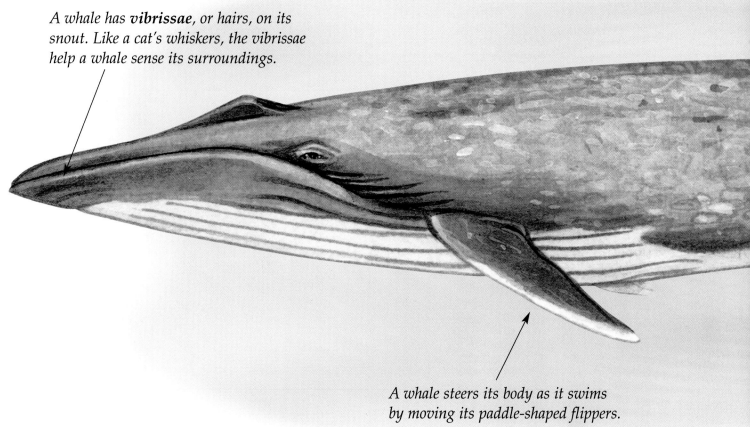

*A whale has **vibrissae**, or hairs, on its snout. Like a cat's whiskers, the vibrissae help a whale sense its surroundings.*

A whale steers its body as it swims by moving its paddle-shaped flippers.

Baleen or teeth?

Toothed whales have sharp teeth, which they use to catch food. To learn how toothed whales catch food, see pages 16 and 17. Baleen whales do not have teeth. Instead, these whales have **baleen** hanging down from their upper jaws. Baleen are long thin plates made of a material called **keratin**. Your fingernails are also made of keratin. To learn how baleen whales catch food using their baleen, see pages 14 and 15.

a dolphin's teeth

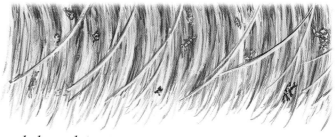

a baleen plate

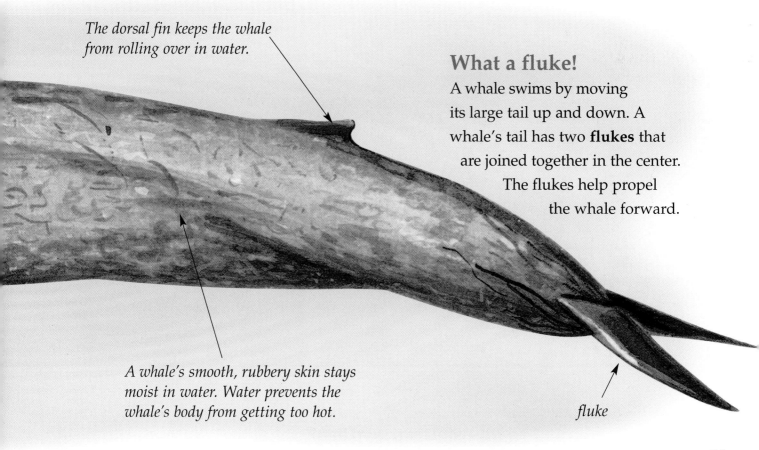

The dorsal fin keeps the whale from rolling over in water.

A whale's smooth, rubbery skin stays moist in water. Water prevents the whale's body from getting too hot.

What a fluke!

A whale swims by moving its large tail up and down. A whale's tail has two **flukes** that are joined together in the center. The flukes help propel the whale forward.

fluke

How do whales breathe?

Whales must breathe air into their lungs to stay alive. They swim to the surface of the water to take breaths of air. A whale breathes using its **blowhole**. A blowhole is an opening at the top of a whale's head. Toothed whales have one blowhole, and baleen whales have two blowholes. When a whale swims to the surface of the water, it opens its blowhole to let out the air in its lungs. The whale then takes in fresh air and closes its blowhole again before diving under water. Once the air is inside the whale's body, it moves to the whale's lungs.

Half asleep

Whales need about eight hours of sleep every day, just as humans do. A whale must always be partially awake in order to breathe, so it allows only one half of its brain to sleep at a time. The dolphin below is floating on the surface of the water while it sleeps.

a toothed whale's blowhole

a baleen whale's blowholes

Storing oxygen

All mammals need to breathe **oxygen** to stay alive. The oxygen moves throughout their bodies in their blood. Whales have more blood than other mammals have. Having more blood means that whales can store more oxygen in their bodies than other mammals can. As a result, whales do not need to breathe as often as do other mammals.

"Thar she blows"

When whales breathe out, **vapor** shoots out of their blowholes. Vapor is a mist made up of tiny water droplets. The vapor is created when the warm air leaving the whale's body hits the cold air above the water. The same thing happens when you exhale and see your breath on a cold winter day.

This blue whale is blowing vapor into the air. A whale can blow vapor up to thirteen feet (4 m) into the air!

Baleen whales

Baleen whales have huge bodies, so they need to eat a lot! They eat mainly **plankton**. Plankton are **microscopic** plants and animals that float in oceans. They are so small and lightweight that they cannot swim. Waves move plankton throughout the oceans. Most baleen whales also eat **krill**. Krill are tiny shrimplike animals. As well, a few species of baleen whales eat fish such as herring, mackerel, and capelin.

krill

plankton

mackerel

Solitary animals

Baleen whales are **filter feeders**. Filter feeders are animals that eat by **filtering**, or straining, bits of food from water. Filter feeders do not need help from other animals to catch food, so baleen whales are mainly **solitary animals**. Solitary animals usually live and find food alone. Baleen whales use three different types of filter feeding: **skim feeding**, **gulp feeding**, and **bottom feeding**.

Skimming dinner

Right whales are mainly skim feeders. Skim feeding takes place at, or just beneath, the ocean's surface. To skim feed, a right whale swims forward with its mouth open. Water flows into the front of its mouth and comes out at the sides. As the water flows through the whale's mouth, food gets stuck in the whale's baleen. This southern right whale is skim feeding.

The big gulp

Rorqual whales, including humpbacks, minkes, and blue whales, are mainly gulp feeders. They feed within 328 feet (100 m) of the water's surface. To gulp feed, a rorqual whale swims quickly into a **school**, or group, of **prey**. The whale then opens its mouth and takes in a huge gulp of water. **Ventral pleats** on the whale's neck expand to make room for the water. Once the prey are inside the whale's mouth, the whale closes its mouth and uses its tongue to push out the water. Krill and other food get stuck in the whale's baleen as the water is pushed out. The whale then swallows the prey.

This blue whale has gulped a huge amount of water. Its ventral pleats have expanded to make room. Bubbles form as the whale pushes out the water.

Bottom feeders

Gray whales bottom feed mainly in coastal waters that are between thirteen and 394 feet (4 to 120 m) deep. To bottom feed, a gray whale rolls to one side on the ocean floor and sucks in a large amount of water and mud. The whale then pushes the water and mud out the sides of its mouth, and the prey gets trapped in the whale's baleen. The whale now swallows the prey. The gray whale, shown right, is dragging its body along the ocean floor to loosen the mud before it feeds.

15

Toothed whales

Whales are **predators**, or animals that hunt and kill other animals for food. Unlike baleen whales, toothed whales dive deep into oceans to catch prey. Toothed whales are fast swimmers. They use their speed to chase and capture fast-moving prey. Toothed whales use their sharp teeth to grab prey and to tear it apart. Some also swallow prey whole. Toothed whales eat fish, squid, shellfish, and even sea birds. Orcas are the only whales that eat other marine mammals. Orcas may hunt seals, sea lions, porpoises, and dolphins.

Social animals

Toothed whales are **social animals**. Social animals live and find food in groups. Toothed whales are social animals because they cannot capture enough food on their own to survive. They live in groups of different sizes. The size of a group depends on the type of prey the whales eat. Whales that hunt large schools of fish often live in large groups. Whales that dive deep to find food, or those that hunt prey that travel long distances, live in small groups. Most narwhals, shown above, live in small groups of five to ten whales.

Echoes through the water

Most toothed whales use **echolocation** to find food and to learn about their surroundings. Echolocation helps whales locate objects using **echoes**. Echoes are waves of sound. A whale echolocates by making clicking noises. These noises travel away from the whale, bounce off objects, and return to the whale as echoes. The echoes create a picture in the whale's brain, which allows the whale to "see" the objects around itself.

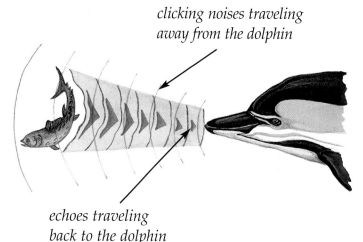

clicking noises traveling away from the dolphin

echoes traveling back to the dolphin

How do whales echolocate?

To echolocate, a toothed whale, such as a dolphin, creates a series of clicking sounds in its **nasal passage**. The nasal passage is located inside the dolphin's blowhole. The sounds travel from the nasal passage into the dolphin's **melon**. The melon is a fatty part in the dolphin's head. The dolphin uses its melon to direct the sounds toward an object. Once the sounds reach the object, they bounce back to the dolphin's brain, "showing" the dolphin the size, shape, and location of the object. Echolocation allows dolphins and other toothed whales to know if the objects around them are food. It also keeps the whales from swimming into objects or other animals in the ocean. The dolphins on the right are using echolocation to find fish beneath the sand. They will use their snouts to dig up the fish.

Whale noises

Whales **communicate** with one another in different ways. To communicate means to send and receive messages. Whales communicate mainly by making different sounds. All whales have excellent hearing, which helps them hear sounds under water.

Noises in the ocean can affect the way whales communicate. For example, belugas, such as the one shown above, make noises when they hear ships. When narwhals hear ships, however, they stop making noises.

Toothed whale noises

Toothed whales make many kinds of sounds, including barks, squeaks, whistles, clicks, and cries. Toothed whales may make whistling and clicking noises to let other whales know that predators or prey are nearby. They may also use sounds as a way of playing. Some species, such as bottlenose dolphins, have **signature whistles**. Signature whistles are whistling sounds that dolphins make. Each dolphin's signature whistle is different. The whistles help dolphins identify one another by their sounds.

Pilot whales usually travel in large groups of 20 to 90 whales. They often make sounds to keep the members of their groups together.

Songs of the sea

Baleen whales make a greater variety of sounds than toothed whales do. These sounds may be greetings, warnings, noises that keep track of baby whales, or calls that attract other whales. Only baleen whales create **songs**.

A baleen whale's song is a series of sounds, such as moans, chirps, squeaks, and sighs, which are repeated in a pattern. At least two species of baleen whales sing, but the most famous songs are performed by male humpback whales, such as the one shown below.

Mating songs

Male humpback whales sing in winter. Scientists are not sure why male humpbacks sing, but most believe that the whales sing to attract female humpbacks for the purpose of **mating**. Mating means joining together to make babies.

Male humpbacks sing songs only in their **mating grounds**. Mating grounds are the areas of the ocean where whales mate. A humpback song can last from five to 30 minutes. Some whales sing for only a few minutes. Others sing song after song for as long as two days.

Whale moves

Whales also communicate using movements. Many whales are affectionate with one another. They touch and rub each other with their heads, fins, and the sides of their bodies. Some whales, especially dolphins, are playful and outgoing. A few of the ways in which whales move are shown on these two pages.

*A whale **spyhops**, or lifts its head out of the water, to look around above the surface of the ocean.*

*Whales often **breach**, or leap high out of the water. They may breach out of fear or anger or to loosen **parasites** on their skin.*

*Dolphins often **porpoise**. To porpoise is to move quickly forward by leaping out of the water.*

*Whales sometimes rest by **logging**, or lying motionless at the surface of the water. Parts of their bodies, such as their backs or heads, are usually exposed to the air as they rest.*

*Whales such as humpbacks **fin-slap** by hitting their large flippers against the surface of the water. Whales may fin-slap when they are trying to scare away predators.*

Too close for comfort

Whales sometimes compete with one another for food, mating partners, or home ranges. Young males tend to be the most aggressive whales. Toothed whales fight by biting or by hitting one another with their jaws or tails. Male sperm whales may also ram their heads together. Male baleen whales threaten other male whales with fearsome displays. Scientists believe these displays are ways of competing for mating partners. Displays may include breaching, **lobtailing**, singing, and blowing bubbles.

When a whale lobtails, it swings its tail around in the air and then slaps it against the water's surface.

Whale migrations

Most species of baleen whales **migrate**. To migrate means to travel from one place to another for a certain period of time. Many baleen whales have two home ranges. One is in the polar or temperate waters where the whales usually live. The other home range is thousands of miles away, in the tropical oceans to which the whales migrate each year.

Long journeys

For most of the year, baleen whales live in polar and temperate oceans, where there is plenty of food. They eat a lot to add blubber to their bodies. In winter, the baleen whales migrate to warm waters to mate and to have babies. There are fewer predators in warm waters, so the babies are safer there than they are in the cold waters. There is not much food in warm waters, however. While they are in their mating grounds, the adult whales do not eat. They live off the blubber in their bodies. In spring, they return to the polar or temperate oceans.

Gray whales make the longest migration of any mammal. They travel between 5,000 and 7,000 miles (8047 and 11 265 km) each way!

Traveling toothed whales

Very few species of toothed whales migrate. The sperm whale is the only toothed whale that migrates long distances. Most toothed whales that migrate travel only to follow prey animals that migrate. For example, many orcas, such as the ones shown below, eat salmon. Each year, the orcas follow the migrating salmon.

Scientists are not sure how whales find their way across many miles of ocean waters year after year. Some scientists believe that when migrating whales spyhop, they may be looking for familiar sights.

Whale babies

After adult baleen whales mate in tropical waters, they return to their home ranges in polar or temperate oceans. **Calves**, or babies, develop inside the bodies of the female whales for about ten to twelve months, while the whales are in the cold waters. When the mother whales migrate again to their mating grounds the following year, they give birth to their calves.

Toothed whale babies

Toothed whales mate and have their calves in their usual home ranges. Different species of toothed whales mate and have calves at different times of the year. Baby toothed whales develop inside the bodies of their mothers for seven to seventeen months.

Calves stay close to their mothers, as this blue whale calf is doing. Mother whales protect their babies from predators.

A whale is born

Most species of baleen and toothed whales give birth to only one calf at a time. Another female whale sometimes assists a mother whale that is giving birth. The assistant may use her mouth to help pull the baby out of the mother's body. A calf is born tailfirst. The mother whale pushes her baby to the water's surface immediately, so it can take its first breath, as shown right. The calf can swim as soon as it is born.

Nursing

Calves **nurse**, or drink milk from the bodies of their mothers. Mother whales have **mammary slits**, or openings that contain nipples. To nurse, a calf curls its tongue around a nipple, forming a tube. The mother whale uses her muscles to squirt milk into the calf's mouth through the tube. Every so often, the calf stops nursing and swims up to the surface of the water to breathe. Calves nurse for six months to two years, depending on the species. Some calves gain up to 220 pounds (100 kg) per day! When calves start hunting prey, they stray farther and farther from their mothers.

Whales in the food web

To survive, all living things need energy. Animals get energy by eating plants or other animals. This pattern of eating and being eaten is called a **food chain**. When two or more food chains connect, a **food web** is formed. A food web that includes whales is shown on these pages. The arrows point toward the living things that are receiving energy. For example, the web shows a seal receiving energy by eating krill, and an orca receiving energy by eating the seal.

humpback whale

anchovies

Pacific white-sided dolphin

orca

squid

harp seal

krill

lobster

clams

plankton

Dangers to whales

oil rig

*Noise caused by **oil rigs**, fishing, and large ships travels through oceans. This noise disturbs whales and can damage their hearing.*

Whales are in danger because their **populations** are getting smaller. A population is the total number of one type of animal living in a certain area. People threaten whale populations by **over-hunting**, or killing too many, whales and by harming the environment. Two ways that people harm the environment are by destroying habitats and by causing **global warming**.

Over-hunting

Over-hunting is the reason that many whales are endangered. During the 1900s, millions of whales were killed for their meat, blubber, and baleen. Blubber is boiled and made into a type of oil. Until the 1930s, baleen was used to make products such as umbrellas, brooms, and brushes. Today, there are international laws that prevent too many whales from being hunted. Norway is the only country that still has a **commercial** whaling industry. Norway continues to allow people to hunt minke whales.

Sea of pollution

People destroy whale habitats by polluting the environment. When oil leaks or spills from ships, whales may eat it or suck it into their blowholes. The oil makes the whales sick. Chemicals that are dumped into oceans also build up in plants and in the bodies of animals. When whales eat these plants or animals, the whales are also poisoned. Whales may also become tangled up in garbage and old fishing nets that are thrown into oceans. The dolphin below is tangled in a fishing net.

Global warming

Over time, pollution and other environmental damage have caused global warming. Global warming is a gradual rise in the Earth's temperature. Scientists are not sure what the long-term effects of global warming will be, but even small changes to the environment can harm wildlife. For example, scientists believe that the rise in the Earth's temperature has decreased the amount of plankton in the Arctic Ocean. With less plankton, baleen whales may soon have trouble finding enough food to eat.

Learning more

Scientists are always trying to learn more about how whales live, find food, raise their babies, and communicate. The more people know about whales, the better they can help them survive. Whales take up to ten years to become **mature**. Mature whales are whales that can have babies. When whales are killed before they can have babies, they cannot add to whale populations. People need to work together to protect whales, especially endangered whales. Some species of endangered whales include blue whales, bowhead whales, fin whales, humpback whales, Hector's dolphins, and sperm whales.

How many whales?

Scientists count whales to ensure that their populations are healthy. Counting whales is a difficult task because whales are always on the move! By visiting areas where whales usually feed, researchers can count a lot of whales without having to travel all over the world. Researchers use a few tricks to make sure they do not count the same whales more than once. For example, the markings on a humpback's tail, shown above, are as unique as human fingerprints are. Each blue whale also has a different color pattern on its dorsal fin.

Whale watching

Millions of people go whale watching each year. Tourists head out on oceans in kayaks, motorboats, and other vessels to see whales up close. The whale-watching industry makes almost one billion dollars each year! This is good news for whales because communities that depend on whale watching are helping ensure that whales are protected. Whale watchers can disturb whales, however. Whales are disturbed when too many boats are in the water at once, or when the boats move too close to the animals.

Whale watchers are fascinated by seeing these giant marine mammals up close. Sometimes whales also seem fascinated by the whale watchers!

Glossary

Note: Boldfaced words that are defined in the text may not appear in the glossary.

baleen Long plates found in a baleen whale's mouth, which are used for filter feeding

coastal Ocean waters that are close to shore

commercial Describing work that is done to make money

endangered Describing animals that are in danger of disappearing from the Earth forever

extinct Describing a plant or an animal that no longer exists on Earth

global warming A gradual rise in the Earth's temperature

microscopic Describing plants and animals that are so small that they can only be seen with a microscope

oxygen A gas in air and water that animals must breathe to stay alive

parasite A living thing that feeds off an animal's body

polar oceans Cold oceans that are located at the North Pole or at the South Pole

prey Animals that are hunted and eaten by other animals

tropical oceans Warm oceans that are located at the equator

ventral pleats Long grooves on a baleen whale's neck that expand during feeding to make room for water

Index

1 2 3 4 5 6 7 8 9 0 Printed in the U.S.A. 4 3 2 1 0 9 8 7 6 5